GEOGRAPHY OF THE WORLD

ANTARCTICA

By Dana Meachen Rau

THE CHILD'S WORLD®
CHANHASSEN, MINNESOTA

The
Child's
World®

Published in the United States of America by The Child's World®
P.O. Box 326, Chanhassen, MN 55317-0326
800-599-READ
www.childsworld.com

Photo Credits: Cover: Pablo Corral Vega/Corbis; Animals Animals/Earth Scenes: 7
(Ben Osborne/OSF), Corbis:11 (Robert Weight), 20, 21 (Hulton-Deutsch Collection),
27 (Gary Braasch); Doug Allan/OSF/Animals Animals/Earth Scenes: 15, 17; Galen
Rowell/Corbis: 4, 25; Travelsite/Picture Desk: 6; Travelsite/Global/Picture Desk: 8, 14,
23; Wolfgang Kaehler/Corbis: 18, 19.

The Child's World®: Mary Berendes, Publishing Director
Editorial Directions, Inc.: E. Russell Primm, Editorial Director; Pam Rosenberg, Line
Editor; Katie Marsico, Assistant Editor; Olivia Nellums, Editorial Assistant; Susan
Hindman, Copy Editor; Elizabeth K. Martin, Proofreader; Ann Grau Duvall, Peter
Garnham, Carol Yehling, Fact Checkers; Dr. Charles Maynara, Professor of Geography,
Radford University, Radford, Virginia, Subject Consultant; Tim Griffin/IndexServ,
Indexer; Cian Loughlin O'Day, Photo Researcher; Elizabeth K. Martin, Photo Selector;
XNR Productions, Inc., Cartographer

Library of Congress Cataloging-in-Publication Data
Rau, Dana Meachen, 1971–
  Antarctica / by Dana Meachen Rau.
    p. cm. — (Our galaxy and beyond)
Summary: Describes the basic geography, topography, history, plant and animal life,
and climate of Antarctica. Includes bibliographical references and index.
  ISBN 1-59296-064-2 (Library Bound : alk. paper)
  1. Antarctica—Juvenile literature. [1. Antarctica.] I. Title. II. Series.
  G863.R38 2004
  919.8'9—dc21   2003008035

TABLE OF CONTENTS

CHAPTER ONE

WHERE IS ANTARCTICA?

globe of the Earth can be divided into two parts when split

across its middle—the Northern **Hemisphere** and the

Southern Hemisphere. The northernmost and southernmost parts

of the globe are called its poles. Antarctica is found in the Southern

Hemisphere surrounding the South Pole. It lies between 60 degrees

south **latitude** and 90 degrees south latitude. The Arctic is the area

Mount Lister is part of the Transantarctic mountain range,
which runs the entire length of the continent.

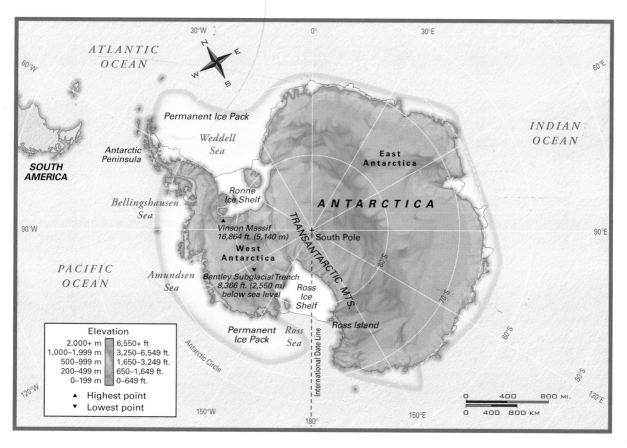

A physical map of Antarctica

around the North Pole. Antarctica means "the opposite of the Arctic."

Antarctica is an **island.** The Atlantic Ocean, Indian Ocean,

and Pacific Ocean surround Antarctica. The southern parts of these

oceans are also considered a separate ocean, called the Southern or

Antarctic Ocean.

The mainland of Antarctica is made up of East Antarctica and

West Antarctica. The Antarctic **Peninsula** curves northward from

West Antarctica. There are also various islands scattered around

Antarctica's coast. A mountain range called

the Transantarctic Mountains divides East

and West Antarctica.

Glaciers cover almost all of

Antarctica. One large ice sheet covers the

Glaciers run down the Airdevronsix Icefalls into a dry valley, reshaping Antarctica's landscape.

Sometimes large pieces of glaciers break off in the ocean and become icebergs.
These tabular icebergs look like big table tops.

land of East Antarctica. Another sheet covers West Antarctica.

Scientists believe that not all of West Antarctica is above sea level. So

if the West Antarctic ice sheet ever melted, the land would be made up

of islands. The ice of Antarctica is from 1 to 3 miles (1.6 to 4.8 kilo-

meters) thick.

CLOSEST COUNTRIES

New Zealand, an island near Australia, and Chile, on the tip of South America, are the countries closest to Antarctica. People traveling to Antarctica first go to New Zealand or Chile, and then take a plane or boat to Antarctica.

The icebreaker ship Molchanov *glides through the Lemaire Channel on its way to a research station.*

The coast of the continent, where glaciers float on the ocean, is called an ice shelf. Antarctica has two very large ice shelves—the Ronne Ice Shelf and the Ross Ice Shelf. Sometimes, pieces of the ice shelves break off. This is called calving. The pieces of ice that break off are called icebergs. They float in the sea around Antarctica.

CHAPTER TWO

How Did Antarctica Come to Be?

Antarctica is one of seven large areas of land on Earth. These areas of land are called continents. The other continents are Asia, Africa, North America, South America, Europe, and Australia. Antarctica is the fifth-largest continent.

> **HOW BIG IS ANTARCTICA?**
> Antarctica is about 5.4 million square miles (14 million sq km). That is about the same area as the United States and Mexico together.

Antarctica is very different from the other continents. All the other continents are filled with people, animals, and plants. There are cities, farms, neighborhoods, and parks. But Antarctica is so cold that no people have ever settled there to live.

How was Antarctica formed? About 135 million years ago, some of the continents were clumped together to make three large areas of land on Earth. One of these pieces of land was called Gondwanaland.

It included the present-day continents of South America, Africa, Antarctica, and Australia, as well as the Indian **subcontinent.**

About 45 million years ago, Gondwanaland split apart, and the continents moved to the positions they are in today. Antarctica's position is at the most southern point of Earth, where it is very cold.

Antarctica was not always so cold. Scientists know this because they have found **fossils** of warm-weather plants, trees, and animals in Antarctica. When Antarctica was part of Gondwanaland, it was further north, where it was warmer. It was a continent with mountains and lowlands, much like the others. Then, about 38 million years ago, glaciers began to cover Antarctica. Today, the continent is almost completely covered by ice.

FOSSILS

Fossils are the remains of animals or plants. A fossil is formed when an animal or plant is quickly buried by mud or sand and minerals in the ground turn it into stone. Scientists use fossils to see what life was like long ago.

CHAPTER THREE

WHAT MAKES
ANTARCTICA SPECIAL?

Antarctica is the coldest place on Earth. Usually, the temperature there is between −90° Fahrenheit (−68°Celsius) and 32°F (0°C). The lowest temperature ever recorded on Earth was in Antarctica. It was −129°F (−89°C). Antarctica is also the windiest place on Earth.

A small airplane brings supplies to researchers stationed in the Shackleton Mountains.

Wind blows up to 200 miles (322 km) per hour across the continent.

For half of the year, sunlight shines on Antarctica. The sun never sets in the sky. It is bright even in the middle of the night. The other half of the year, the sky is dark. For about six months, the Sun never shines. This happens because of the way Earth is tilted toward the Sun. During this dark period, Antarctica is especially cold. It is Antarctica's winter. Winter there occurs from about May to September. This is the opposite of winter in the Northern Hemisphere. When the Sun reappears in the sky, winter ends and the ice begins to melt. Antarctica warms to its highest temperatures in the summer.

During the winter, pack ice surrounds the continent. This is ice that forms on the ocean along the coast. The ice extends the shore-

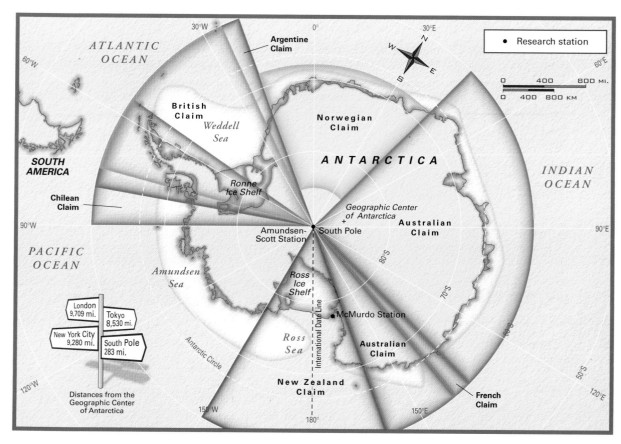

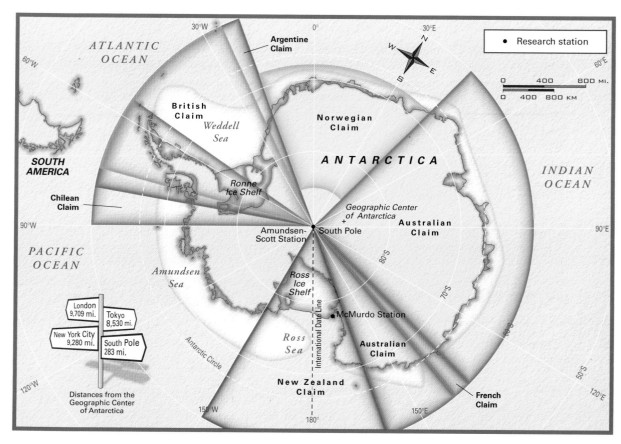

A political map of Antarctica

line of Antarctica up to an extra 1,000 miles (1,600 km). In the

summer, the pack ice melts, and the coast is visible again.

The dry valleys in Antarctica are the only places on the

continent not covered with ice. These areas are deserts. Deserts

are very dry areas of land. Even though Antarctica is not sandy

The aurora australis, or southern lights, light up the Antarctic sky.

THE HIGHEST CONTINENT

Not only is Antarctica the coldest and windiest continent, it is also the highest. It sits about 6,004 feet (1,830 m) above sea level. That is about three times higher than the other continents.

and hot like many deserts on Earth, the valleys are just as dry.

In the darkness of winter, if one looked to the sky above Antarctica, one might see the aurora australis, or southern lights. They are colored lights that seem to dance and ripple across the sky. They are formed by particles of energy from the Sun.

CHAPTER FOUR

WHAT ANIMALS AND PLANTS ARE FOUND IN ANTARCTICA?

Antarctica is so cold and icy that it is hard for animals and plants to live there. **Lichens** are one of the few living things, or organisms, that grow on the land. Lichens grow on rocks in the dry

Lichens, one of the few signs of life on Antarctica, cling to rocks on Signy Island in the South Orkneys.

valleys. Algae grow on the ice, and mosses grow close to the coasts. On the Antarctic Peninsula, where it is a little warmer, there are some grasses.

Only a few animals live on the land. These are insects that can live in the cracks of rocks to protect themselves from the cold and wind. Most of the animals of Antarctica live on the coasts or in the waters around Antarctica.

The ocean is filled with small, shrimplike animals called krill. The seas are also filled with many types of fish and squid.

About seven different types of penguins make Antarctica home, including the Adelie, Chinstrap, and Emperor. Unlike most birds, penguins do not fly. Their wings are made for swimming. To stay warm, they have waterproof feathers that can hold warm air close to

Seals and their young swim between the vast number of glaciers that fill the Antarctic seas.

their bodies. Most penguins leave Antarctica in the winter and travel

north where it is warmer.

Seals also swim in Antarctica's waters. They have a layer of fat,

called blubber, under their skin to keep them warm. Elephant seals,

fur seals, and five other species rest on the ice and swim in the sea.

Most of the seals travel north during the winter. But the Weddell seal

stays in Antarctica all year long. It lives under the ice in the water. It

gets air by biting out a breathing hole in the ice.

Whales come to visit Antarctica in the summer. Minke whales, blue whales, and many others feed along Antarctica's coasts.

Birds also fill the sky. Skuas, petrels, and albatrosses are a few types. The Arctic tern visits Antarctica each summer from as far away as the North Pole!

An orca, or killer whale, near the Antarctic Peninsula during its trek around the world

A black-browed albatross fishes over the rough Antarctic seas. Some albatrosses make long journeys to nest and mate in Antarctica.

The animals of Antarctica all depend on each other. Fish, seabirds, seals, penguins, and some whales feed on krill. Some seals also eat penguins. Some whales also eat seals. The relationship between animals that feed on each other is called a food web. Without each other, the animals could not survive.

CHAPTER FIVE

WHO LIVES IN ANTARCTICA?

Other continents have had people living on them for centuries. The first recorded landings on Antarctica were not until the 1800s.

For a long time, people believed that there might be land near the South Pole. Some sailed near it but never landed on it. British explorer Captain James Cook was the first to cross the Antarctic Circle, in 1773. In 1823, British navigator James Weddell sailed even farther south than Cook had. Charles Wilkes, Jules d'Urville, and Sir James Ross discovered and charted many parts of the continent in three separate voyages between 1838 and 1843.

In 1911, two parties of explorers began

James Cook traveled around the world and braved the great Ice Islands that we now know as Antarctica.

Robert Scott reaches the tent of fellow explorer Roald Amundsen in 1912. Amundsen and his team beat Scott to the South Pole by about one month.

the trip across Antarctica to reach

the South Pole. Norwegian Roald

Amundsen and his team reached the

South Pole on December 14, 1911, and returned home safely. When

Robert Scott, an English explorer, and his men reached the South Pole

on January 16, 1912, they were surprised and disappointed to see that

Amundsen reached the South Pole before them. Then, sadly, Scott and his men died on the return journey.

More people explored the continent on foot and by air. Countries began claiming parts of Antarctica for their own. Then in 1957 and 1958, scientists from 12 different countries came to Antarctica to set up research stations. They studied Antarctica and fully mapped the continent.

In 1959, **representatives** from the 12 countries got together to sign a **treaty.** It said that countries could not claim parts of Antarctica. It also said that Antarctica was only to be used for peaceful reasons. The representatives agreed that it would be a place for research. Scientists who studied Antarctica would share their scientific information with scientists from all other countries. These 12 countries, and many others that have joined them, have been working

Researchers cross the Neumayer Glacier. They wear the best gear to stay warm and bring lots of supplies in case they lose their way.

THE INTERNATIONAL TRANS-ANTARCTICA EXPEDITION
In 1990, a team of six men from around the world was the first to cross Antarctica by dogsled. It was called the International Trans-Antarctica Expedition.

together since 1959 to keep Antarctica a peaceful place for scientists to work.

Today, people live in Antarctica on research stations all over the continent. About 4,000 people live there in the summer and about 1,000 in winter.

CHAPTER SIX

WHAT IS ANTARCTICA LIKE TODAY?

Many countries have set up permanent stations across Antarctica designed to do scientific research. Today, there are about 40 permanent research stations on Antarctica. In addition, there are about 25 stations that are set up only in the summer.

People who live and work at the stations must find ways to adapt to the cold weather. Each person must bring a heavy coat, waterproof pants, many pairs of mittens and gloves, fleece pants and jackets, flannel shirts, long underwear, wool socks, and boots.

The permanent research stations are like small towns. McMurdo Station on Ross Island is the largest U.S. research station. It

TOURISTS
Researchers are not the only people who travel to Antarctica. From 12,000 to 15,000 people visit Antarctica each year as tourists. They usually arrive by ship and visit Antarctic sites for about two weeks.

has places for people to sleep, a cafeteria, churches, and stores. It has a runway for planes to land. Amundsen-Scott Station is another U.S. station. It is at the South Pole. The buildings of this station are under a huge dome that helps protect them from Antarctica's weather. When researchers need to get from one place to the other, they travel by helicopters, snowmobiles, **Sprytes,** on skis, or on foot.

The Amundsen-Scott research base is named for the first two men to reach the South Pole and uses the newest technology to make Antarctica livable for scientists.

Many kinds of science are studied on Antarctica. Some scientists study the land and ice. Some study the weather. Some study glaciers and the way they move. Some study the oceans and the animals that live there. Some of the scientists are astronomers who use telescopes to study outer space.

Antarctica does have problems. One is the amount of garbage. Because so many people live and work there, they need to find good ways to dispose of their trash. Another big problem lies above Antarctica in the ozone layer. Ozone is a gas in the Earth's atmosphere. It protects Earth from some of the Sun's harmful rays. Air pollution created by people all over the world is making a hole in the ozone layer above Antarctica. The Sun's rays are breaking through and killing the tiny organisms in the water that krill feed on. If the krill do not survive, the food web made up of all the animals in Antarctica will be affected.

Countries around the world and the researchers in Antarctica are doing what they can to keep Antarctica a peaceful place to study. They want to learn more about this icy continent at the South Pole.

A researcher explores an ice cave in the Marr Glacier, one of the many wonders of Antarctica.

Glossary

fossils (FOSS-uhls) Fossils are the remains of plants and animals from millions of years ago.

glaciers (GLAY-shurs) Glaciers are huge sheets of ice.

hemisphere (HEM-uhss-fihr) One half of a sphere—such as the northern half or southern half of Earth when it is divided in two by the equator—is called a hemisphere.

island (EYE-luhnd) An island is a piece of land surrounded by water.

latitude (LAT-uh-tood) Latitude is the position of a place on the globe as it is measured in degrees north or south of the equator.

lichens (LYE-kens) Lichens are fungi and algae that live together as one organism.

meteorites (MEE-tee-ur-rites) Meteorites are pieces of rock from space that fall to Earth without burning up in Earth's atmosphere.

peninsula (puh-NIN-suh-luh) A peninsula is a piece of land that sticks out from a larger piece of land and is almost completely surrounded by water.

representatives (rep-ri-ZEN-tuh-tivs) Representatives are people who have been chosen to speak or make decisions for others.

Sprytes (SPRITES) Sprytes are large vehicles with tracks like a bulldozer.

subcontinent (SUB-KON-tih-nent) A subcontinent is a large landmass that is smaller than a continent and often part of a continent.

treaty (TREE-tee) A treaty is a written agreement between two or more nations or groups of people.

An Antarctic Almanac

Location on the Globe:
Latitude: 60° south to 90° south
(the South Pole)

Greatest distance: 3,450 miles
(5,550 km)

Borders: Atlantic Ocean, Indian Ocean,
Pacific Ocean

Total Area: 5,400,000 square miles
(14,000,000 sq km)

Highest Point: Vinson Massif,
16,864 feet (5,140 km) above sea level

Lowest Point: Bentley Subglacial
Trench, 8,366 feet (2,550 m) below sea level

Major Mountain Ranges:
Antarctic Peninsula, Ellsworth, Prince
Charles, Transantarctic, Whitmore

Major Glaciers: Beardmore,
Lambert, Rennick, Support Force

Countries that maintain research stations on Antarctica:

Argentina	Japan
Australia	New Zealand
Brazil	Norway
Bulgaria	Poland
Chile	Russia
China	South Africa
Finland	South Korea
France	Spain
Germany	Ukraine
Great Britain	United States
India	Uruguay
Italy	

Population (researchers):
About 4,000 in summer
About 1,000 in winter

Antarctica in the News

38 million B.C.	Glaciers begin to form in Antarctica.
13 million B.C.	The Antarctic ice sheet begins forming.
5 million B.C.	Almost all of Antarctica is covered by the Antarctic ice sheet.
A.D. 100s	Greek geographer Ptolemy, believing that there must be a large land mass at Earth's south end in order to balance out the northern land masses, names this unknown land mass Terra Australis Incognita, or Unknown Southern Land.
1772	British explorer Captain James Cook begins a search for the unknown southern continent. In 1774 he is the first person to cross the Antarctic Circle.
1823	British navigator James Weddell sails further south than Cook did.
1838 – 1843	In three separate voyages, Charles Wilkes, Jules d'Urville, and Sir James Ross discover and chart many parts of the continent.
1895	Norwegian Henryk Johan Bull makes the first known landing on the Antarctic mainland.
1901 – 1904	A team led by British explorer Robert Falcon Scott makes the first inland exploration of Antarctica.
1911	Roald Amundsen, a Norwegian explorer, is the first person to reach the South Pole.
1912	Captain Robert F. Scott, leader of a British team of explorers, is disappointed to discover that Amundsen and his team reached the South Pole before he did.
mid-1900s	Richard Byrd, a U.S. Navy officer, leads explorations that increase interest in the study of Antarctica.
1957 – 1958	Scientists from 12 different countries set up research stations on Antarctica and fully map the continent.
1959	Representatives from the 12 countries agree that the continent of Antarctica should be used mainly for research and not claimed by any one country. They sign the Antarctic Treaty.
1983	The world's lowest temperature (-128.6° F, -89.2° C) is recorded at Vostok Station on July 21.
2002	Scientists report that large pieces of the Larsen Ice Shelf in Antarctica are breaking off more rapidly than usual, possibly as a result of overall global warming.

How to Learn More about Antarctica

At the Library

Hooper, Meredith. *Antarctic Adventure: Exploring the Frozen South.*
New York: DK Publishing, 2000.

Peterson, David. *Antarctica.* New York: Children's Press, 1999.

Sayre, April Pulley. *Antarctica.* Brookfield, Conn.: Twenty-First Century Books, 1998.

Webb, Sophie. *My Season with Penguins: An Antarctic Journal.*
New York: Houghton Mifflin, 2000.

On the Web

Visit our home page for lots of links about Antarctica:
http://www.childsworld.com/links.html
Note to Parents, Teachers, and Librarians: We routinely verify our Web links to make sure they're safe, active sites—so encourage your readers to check them out!

Places to Visit or Contact

NATIONAL SCIENCE FOUNDATION
To write for information about Antarctic research
sponsored by the National Science Foundation
Office of Polar Programs
Room 755
4201 Wilson Boulevard
Arlington, VA 22230
703/292-8030

SCOTT POLAR RESEARCH INSTITUTE
To visit their museum and see polar artifacts or
to write for more information about polar topics
University of Cambridge
Lensfield Road
Cambridge CB2 1ER
England
+44 (0)1223 336540

Index

About the Author

Dana Meachen Rau is a children's book author, editor, and illustrator. She has written more than 70 books, including nonfiction, biographies, early readers, and historical fiction. A graduate of Trinity College in Hartford, Connecticut, Dana is happiest when she is drinking a cup of hot cocoa, sitting on the couch, and holding her pad and pen. She works from her home office in Burlington, Connecticut, where she lives with her husband, Chris, and children, Charlie and Allison.